My First Persian (Farsi)
Alphabets

Picture Book with English Translations

Published By: AuthorUnlock.com

ا

اسب

Horse

ب

بز

Goat

پروانہ

Butterfly

ت

توپ

Ball

ث ت

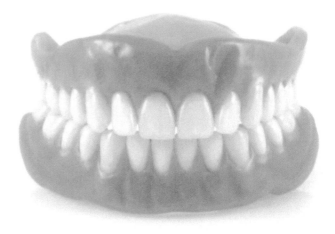

لثه

Gums

ج

جغد

Owl

چ

چتر

Umbrella

ح

حلزون

Snail

خ

خوک

Pig

د

درخت

Tree

ذرت

Corn

ر

روباه

Fox

ز

زنبور

Bee

ث

ژله

Jelly

س س

سگ

Dog

ث

شتر

Camel

ص

صندلی

Chair

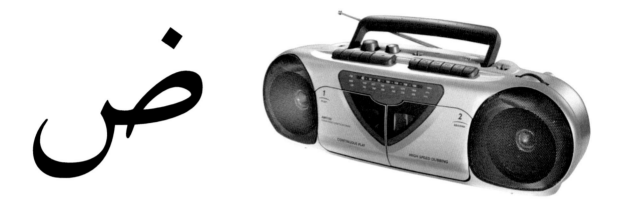

ض

ضبط صوت

Tape recorder

ط

طوطى

Parrot

ظ

ظرف

Dish

ع

عینک

Glasses

غ

غلغلک

Tickle

ف

فيل

Elephant

ق

قورباغه

Frog

ک

کلاغ

Crow

گ گ

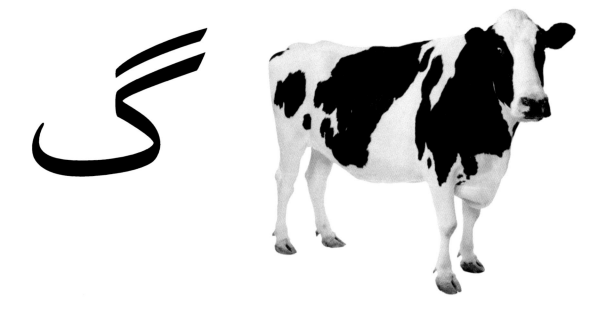

گاو

Cow

ل

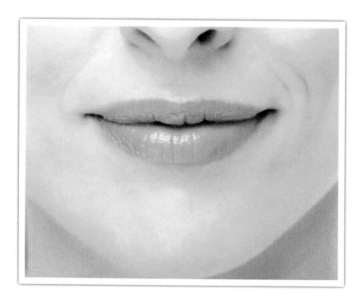

لب

Lips

مرغ

Hen

ن

نان

Bread

و

ويولن

Violin

٥

هويج

Carrot

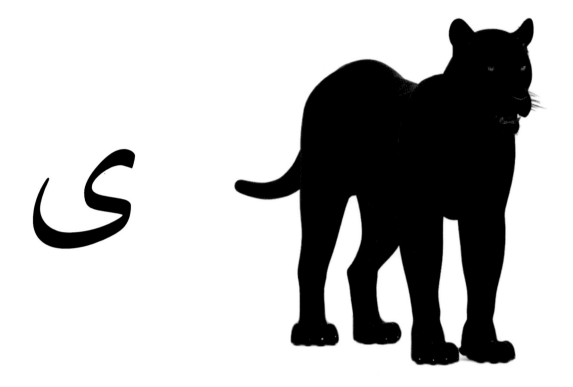

ى

یوزپلنگ

Panther

Made in the USA
Coppell, TX
06 December 2019

12501581R00021